Send Me The Sun And Moon Your Way

Irem Navidakhtar

BookLeaf Publishing

India | USA | UK

Made with ❤ on the BookLeaf Publishing Platform
www.bookleafpub.in
www.bookleafpub.com

Dedication

"Everyone, when they are young, knows what their Personal Legend is.
At that point in their lives, everything is clear and everything is possible.
They are not afraid to dream, and to yearn for everything they would like to see happen to them in their lives."

— The Alchemist, Paulo Coelho

Preface

There are moments in life when something calls to us—an idea, a feeling, a shift that feels like it's meant for us.

"Send Me The Sun And Moon Your Way" is a reflection of those moments—quiet, yet transformative. This collection is not just the story of a soul's journey, but a tribute to the stillness, the seeking, and the finding that shape us along the way.

These 25 poems represent the first 25 years of my life, each one a chapter—capturing the moments of growth, waiting, and discovery. Through them, I explore what it means to be both lost and found, to trust and to question. Each poem is a piece of my story, yet it holds truths I believe are universal—truths about love, faith, and the way we move through the world.

Over the years, I've come to realize that life isn't just shaped by grand events, but also by the subtle signs that appear when we least expect them. It's in those quiet moments, those invisible nudges, that our true path reveals itself. This book serves as a reminder to trust in those moments and to find meaning even in the smallest of things. I didn't write these poems to offer answers, but to ask questions—gentle prompts for those who seek, who feel, and who yearn for something deeper. They are for those who believe in the power of the unseen and for those still learning to listen to the language of the soul.

If you've found this book in your hands, it's no accident. The universe has brought you here for a reason. Trust that.

May this collection be your invitation to step into your own journey—to trust the unfolding, to embrace the signs, and to find the treasure that has always been within you.

Acknowledgements

To my family, my friends, and the strangers whose paths crossed mine—thank you for lighting my way in ways both known and unknown.

1. When the world moved, I stayed still

The school bell echoed, the final chime,
children spilled into the streets, lost in time.
A small figure stood alone but still,
watching the world spin with no thought of will.

Across the road, her home stood near,
a simple path, but too much fear.
The road, the cars, the traffic loud,
her heart knew the way, the path felt shroud.

She watched as others left with ease,
a van, a car, a gentle breeze.
There she stayed, not out of delay,
but in the knowing that she couldn't cross today.

She waited, her gaze steady and pure,
as the world moved fast, she stayed secure.
Her feet knew the steps, but her heart wasn't sure,
for some paths need a hand, a sign to reassure.

And then a wave, a gesture clear,
a mother's smile, a voice to hear.
With trust in her eyes, she knew it was time,
the sign she needed, the reason, the rhyme.

2. Until the Universe says okay

In that stillness, there was more to see,
a lesson hidden, so soft, so free.
She knew the path, it was in her sight,
but she couldn't take the step, not yet, not right.

Sometimes the way is clear and near,
but we stand still, gripped by fear.
Not of the road, nor the steps ahead,
but the uncertainty of where we're being led.

We wait, we long, for a sign to appear,
a guiding hand to quell the fear.
For even when the answer's clear to our eyes,
we need a whisper, a nudge, a gentle prize.

The world rushes on, unaware of her pause,
in that moment, she learned the cause.
That life asks for patience, for trust to grow,
sometimes you can't move until the sign says so.

And in the waiting, she saw it unfold,
the universe listens as stories are told.
In silence, the clarity is found,
when you stop, listen, and let it surround.

For there will be times when we know the way,
but we won't move until the universe says "okay."
And in that pause, we learn to be still,
to trust, to wait, to honour the will.

3. The things we let pass through us

Adam, cast from Eden's gentle shade,
to Earth, where suffering's roots are laid.
He, too, sought a life
a life of knowing,
of understanding
what it meant to belong.

Yet in his fall,
he found not loss,
but the unveiling of truth
that life is not in what we take,
but in what we let pass through us.

What is this Earth if not a place to learn?
A place where we gather the wisdom unlearnt
in the stillness of the breeze,
in the quiet hum of the stars,
in the unnoticed curve of the water's touch?

The things we chase are like shadows,
flickering, fading,
as we are drawn to them
perhaps they hold the key.

But the key has been here,
indeed we failed to see,
in the soil beneath our feet,
in the air we breathe,
in the fleeting moments
of grace slipping through our fingers,
swamped with the reality.

Why didnt we see?
We are like Adam
struggling with our choices,
seeking meaning in things
that are destined to return to dust.

4. Did you notice?

Did you notice
the way water curls
around your fingertips
in the morning basin?

How the fruit,
bursting with color,
offered itself to you
without a single word?

Did you watch the lake
shift like emotion,
blue, then grey, then silver,
then still?

Or the tree outside your window,
how it stands,
naked in winter,
and yet, never ashamed?

You see,
the world gives without title.
It blooms for no audience.
It dies and returns
with no promise of applause.

And yet,
we seek more than what is given
more than the tree,
more than the lake,
more than the silent song
of the passing seasons.

We chase things
things that promise us more,
things that carry weight
and status,
things that fill the space
but never the soul.

5. The wind knows us all

The wind whispers softly through the trees,
it touches lives, unseen, with ease.
It brushes past a child's first laugh,
a fleeting joy, like the breeze's path.
It travels on, through busy streets,
Where strangers pass with hurried feet.

A lady stands, her thoughts afar,
her dreams like shadows, chasing the stars.
The wind moves on, across the plains,
it feels the old man's quiet pains.
His heart beats slow, like the setting sun,
and yet, he holds the words unsung.
It soars above a mountain's peak,
where a young boy's hopes are bold but meek.

The wind carries them, soft yet strong,
and in its breeze, they all belong.
It's the same wind, the same sky,
yet in each heart, the questions fly.

What is it to be alive, to dream, to feel?
Is it a mystery, or a sham unreal?
and through the winds, there lies the truth,
in every age, in every youth,
the lives are different, and the paths are wide,
the same breath of life is felt inside.

For the wind, in passing, sees it clear,
the unity of all who are here.
Eight billion souls, each a song,
together they dance, where they belong.

6. The sacred art of stillness

They say I'm wasting time
when I sit,
unmoving,
as the afternoon drips golden down the wall.

But what is time,
if not a thread we keep knotting,
afraid it might unravel into stillness?

I breathe.

I exist.

I let the light pass through me
like wind through lace
and still they say:
"Do something."
But I am.

I am watching

how the shadows shift across the floor,
how silence holds a sound,
too sacred to speak aloud.

I am the page before the poem,
the pause between the notes.
The couch I melt into becomes,
an altar of stillness,
and I, a priest of pause.

What if doing nothing,
is the soul's way
of stretching its limbs?
Of whispering,
"I am here, without effort,
and that is enough."
Let them chase clocks.

Let them run until their names wear thin.
I will be here,
in the soft rebellion
of non-doing.

Drinking time,
not spending it.
Breathing life,
not burning it.

Because maybe,
the deepest becoming
is in the moment
we let ourselves simply,
be.

7. Where two Souls collide

Two souls collide
beneath the star's light,
unseen threads guide,
through day and night.

Love is choosing the grey,
staying through storms that sway,
when the light feels far,
holding tight to the distant star.

A pull unresolved,
through time's embrace,
the earth hums,
in silent grace.

Hearts may wander,
but they remain,
waiting for the moment
when the story will reign.

8. They remember

Eyes do not see
they recall.
each glance,
a memory stirred.
each stare,
a truth once buried,
rising like mist in morning light.
Look long enough,
and the silence within them
shifts the soul,
within them the chapters unfold,
long held quiet,
begins to speak in the language,
only stillness understands.

9. It already knows

The universe speaks in silent tongues,
a language unknown, yet deeply sung.
it watches, listens, and moves with grace,
in every pause, in every space.

Ask, and its response will come,
not in haste, but in perfect sum.
It answers in ways you cannot see,
until you trust, and let it be.

Detach when the weight feels too near,
release, for growth is born from here.
In the stillness, space will form,
where what's meant for you will transform.

The path may twist, the road unclear,
but each step is one you must steer.
Believe in the journey, trust the climb,
for all that's yours is bound in time.

And when you release, when you let go,
you'll find that the universe already knows.

17

10. Where the Dust holds the answer

A thirst not quenched
by water or wine
not hunger of body,
but of something divine.

A silence that sings
in a tongue not mine,
like echoes from stars
in a forgotten line.

The heart leans out,
stretching through space,
reaching for warmth
it cannot trace.

It aches for a name
it has never heard,
for a feeling
without sound,

without word.

A yearning born
from lives before,
etched in bone,
in spirit's core.

And still,
it waits
not in despair,
but in sacred trust,
as if the answer
rides the dust,
that dances
in the golden dusk.

11. Grace in the unseen

When you give thanks for the gifts unseen,
the universe stirs, and secrets unfold.
As the Quran whispers, "Give thanks, and I will grant
you more."
for a grateful heart unlocks the door.
Gratitude is not just words but the essence of the call,
the soul that bows finds heaven in it all.
What you think about, you bring about, *The Secret* said,
and with thankfulness, the universe is led.
In every breath, in silence, be still
the world will respond when your heart is filled,
for the universe hears the quiet plea,
and in return, it sets you free.

12. White petals, spinning wheels

On bicycles, we glided through the winding streets,
summer dresses swaying, the sun's warmth on our feet.
The air was soft, the breeze cool and light,
as we chased white flowers in the afternoon's gentle
light.

The air was filled with laughter, soft and bright,
we climbed the walls, hearts racing with the thrill,
plucking white petals with joy, as time stood still.

I learned then, as I rode those streets,
life is like this what we seek, we meet.
So many colors, so many blooms,
yet the one we desire fills our rooms.

In the chase, we forget what we pass,
but when we find what we long for,
we're the child at last.

The world is full of gifts we can't see,
yet in seeking, we become all we're meant to be.

13. The Bird behind my eyelid

When I close my eyes,
a tiny red dot appears
just a blood cell,
resting on my eyelid.
But if I look closely,
it starts to move,
like a bird
far away in the sky.
It flaps its wings,
getting closer,
but it never really arrives.
It just keeps flying.
And maybe,
as long as that bird keeps flying,
I'll keep going too.
It feels like a sign
something small,
but full of meaning.
Not something to explain,

just something to feel.
Like a quiet reminder
that I'm still moving,
even when I'm still

14. The Eyes that held me

In the sun's embrace and the shadow's pull,
I met the eyes that had seen it all,
the weight of seasons, the taste of rain,
a soul woven with joy and pain.

They spoke without words,
telling stories of forgotten wars,
of laughter lost in empty halls,
of tears that never truly fall.

Those eyes had travelled through storms,
across deserts, through quiet, quiet forms.
I saw the weight of things unsaid,
the battles were fought inside their head.

In that brief, fleeting glance, I knew
they had walked paths, both cracked and new.
Tried to shield, tried to hide,
but their truth couldn't be denied.

And in their stillness, something broke free
I saw you.
And maybe through you,
I saw me.

15. Grace in the unseen

When all is lost, and silence grows,
even when the stars forget their glow,
there lies a path not marked by stone
a pull within, that calls us home.

Not built on sight, nor proof, nor flame,
it whispers not a god, but a name.
A feeling deep, without a face,
yet moves the soul with quiet grace.

What is this faith, this ancient thread,
that binds the living and the dead?
Not chains, but wings
not fear, but flight,
a way to walk when there's no light.

We follow not for heaven's prize,
nor fear of wrath from distant skies.
But for the stillness it brings near,
the knowing heart, the end of fear.

To bow is not to break, but bloom,
a flower opening in a room.
That's dark, and cold, and yet, somehow,
the light arrives we don't know how.

Faith is the art of trust,
that dust returns, but not just dust.
It teaches: even when you fall,
there is a hand that holds it all.

And when the world no longer stays,
When loss consumes the brightest days,
We still remain, with a voice to say
"I believe, though it's far away."

For what is real may fade and rust,
but faith survives because it must.
The strongest truth, the quietest way,
to believe in what does not decay.

So let the soul, in stillness, pray-
"Send me Your unseen light today."
And if I lose the world I've known
Let me still feel I'm not alone.

16. Roots without a Map

They moved her often,
from city to city, room to room,
like pages turned too fast in a story
that never settled on one chapter.

Each time,
she arrived like the wind,
unfamiliar, quiet,
but watching everything.
Children played, names were exchanged,
but she held hers
like a secret in her pocket.

She learned the language
of temporary walls,
the scent of kitchens
not quite her own,
and the weight of being
both guest and ghost.

But somewhere between the leaving
and the staying,
she began to grow,
not in the way you'd expect,
but deeper.
Not upward, but downward,
into the silent earth
of her own self.

With every new goodbye,
her roots whispered,
we've been here before.
We'll do it again.

And she did.
She became the girl who knew the shortcuts,
the ones who smiled at strangers
like she'd known them all her life,
because somehow she had.
She had lived a thousand small lives
inside one skin,
each one learning how to hold space,
how to stay soft without falling apart.

And now,
when the winds blow again,
she doesn't flinch.

She knows her roots
are already searching, already speaking.
Because she has always known
how to stand still,
in places that don't stay still,
like a tree growing in the desert.

17. The asking is becoming

You'll get used to it, eventually.
That's what they say, as if growth comes with a map.
As if one day,
You'll wake up and feel all the pieces fall into place.

But then, you look back and wonder,
How long did it take for me to understand
that every step, even the missteps,
were leading me to the truth of who I am?

That every moment of doubt
was just a door waiting to be opened?

You see, the universe doesn't give you what you want
to leave you wandering.
It gives you what you need.
To shape you into someone,
who can stand tall when the storms pass.

So ask. Ask for what lights you up,

even if the path ahead feels like a maze.
You're unsure you can navigate.
Ask for the strength,
for the clarity,
for the peace you know is yours to claim.

Ask for it.

Ask for it again.

Ask until the world can no longer ignore your heart's
desire.

Until the universe listens,
until you stop waiting
and start living fully,
knowing you are ready for all that's to come.

Ask for it.
Ask for it.

18. It was me all along

How many steps will it take
before you see that every road you walk
is bringing you closer to *yourself?*
That every search for love,
was a search for the pieces you've yet to find?

19. Lavender finds it's way back

One day I walked into a room,
and it had a smell,
the smell of lavender.
It wrapped me in a warmth I hadn't known I missed.
A soulful whisper from the past,
reminding me that even in change,
there's something that stays,
something that always finds its way back.

20. The proof that I was there

I keep the little things-
chocolate wrappers from birthdays,
tickets to special places,
beads from friendship bracelets,
Dried flowers pressed in books.
School notes, college IDs,
drawings from my childhood,
a single earring,
Love letters tied with memories,
coins from around the world,
straws and fruit-shaped erasers.
I hold them all, not as relics,
But as fragments of time,
pieces that remind me,
that I was once there,
and will always carry,
the echoes of those moments with me.

21. A brief pause, from the knowing

Passerby would ask, "Do you feel like jumping high?"
My mind would always answer, "Yes, but only to the sky."
Into the beauty of waiting, as the golden hour arrives,
With pink, red, and white, where every moment thrives.

The rains, the snow, the trees, so crystal clear,
The moon, the stars, the airplanes drawing near.
Dawn and dusk, as street lights softly glow,
On the walkway where silent footsteps flow.

The neighbor, smoking on the balcony's side,
Would speak of marines and the city's wide tide.
"I see the necklace of lights, golden and bright,"
He'd say, watching the buildings reach for the night.
I'd share this with visitors, who'd sigh and agree,
The city lights and the beauty we all see.

"I find pieces of home wherever I roam,"
They'd whisper softly, feeling at home.

But now, I've added new sights to the mix,
The furniture, the mattress, and laundry tricks.

The universe has planted a seed in my soul,
A sapling in a garden, where I'm made whole.
Watering the same earth, but on a new floor,
A balcony view I never saw before.

The purpose remains, but in time, we'll know,
As we wait for the new winds that help us grow.

22. 222

The life I seek was always near,
A whispered dream I couldn't hear.
But was it mine, or gently laid
By unseen hands in silent shade?

Each choice I made, a thread so fine,
Was woven into some design.
Each road I took, though, felt so free,
Was walked before, just not by me.

Was it fate, or was it chance?
A universe in quiet dance?
Or was I swept in others' wake,
No say in which steps I should take?

And still,
I stand with open eyes,
No longer bound by old replies.

The past is done, its echoes cease,

The future waits, a page of peace.
And in this pause, so vast, so true,
For once, I choose what I walk through.

23. I healed honestly, not perfectly

Healing is not a straight path
it twists like ivy along old stone walls,
winds through back alleys of memory,
where echoes still call your name.

It is the quiet return
to childhood songs heard through cracked doors,
the scent of lavender in old notebooks,
the way sun spills on laundry lines at noon.
It is broken glass under bare feet,
followed by soft moss in hidden clearings.
It is tea left to steep too long,
and letters you never sent—but kept.
Healing is not clean.

It is smudged ink and overgrown gardens,
a journal stained with tears and rain,
a name you say softly- less often, with time.
It's lighting a candle just to watch it melt,

folding grief into your pillow each night,
and waking to birdsong that doesn't sting anymore.

It is learning to touch your scars
like reading Braille of your own survival,
knowing the ache in your bones
means you're still dancing.

Healing is not an arrival,
but a steady becoming.
Like rain carving rivers through stone,
slow, patient, holy.

24. I am only 25 now

Why do I write? What's the reason I speak?
Is it for the world, or just to seek
a truth that's mine, but not yet known,
to carve my name in spaces grown?
Do I seek to be seen, to be heard in time,
Or to hear the echoes of my own rhyme?

At 25, the years still unfold,
But what do I truly know, what's been told?
I've learned, yes, but do I understand
the lessons life holds in my hand?
Am I just repeating what's always been,
or breaking the cycle, finding the skin
of truth that's mine, raw and real,
that others, too, may come to feel?

I stand in this moment, yet so far away,
from the person I'll be when I'm gray.
Will I laugh at these lines, this fleeting view,
as I learn again and again what's true?

Will my 50-year-old self smile with grace,
knowing the lessons I've yet to face?
I'm young, yes, and the road's still long,
but is it for validation I write this song?
Or to hear my soul's quiet cry,
to understand the reason why?

Why do I feel so much, yet still so small?
Why do I seek the answers and never stand tall?
At 25, I'm not an expert yet,
but I'm learning to live without regret.
I'm planting seeds, though they're not all sown,
knowing that some truths are still unknown.

So when I'm 50, I'll have more to say,
but for now, I just trust what comes my way.
For life is a dance, not just a rhyme,
it's a question answered in its own time.
And though I write now, and wonder still,
I'll let my soul speak when it's time to fill
the pages with more than I can see,
the story of a person becoming, just like me.

25. The Song of My Soul

I call to the stars, the sun, the moon,
To all the forces that shape my tune.
I am deserving, I am whole,
I trust in my path, I trust in my soul.

With every breath, I breathe in light,
I am strong, I am bright.
I align with my dreams, with purpose and grace,
The universe supports me, I embrace my place.

I am not bound by what I see,
I am a force, just waiting to be.
My heart knows the way, it's free,
I am open to all that's meant for me.

I ask the universe to open wide,
To show me paths, no place to hide.
I trust in the journey, I trust in my flow,
I am grounded in faith, and it only grows.

I claim the future, bold and bright,
I am limitless, I am light.
What I desire, I now declare,
It's already mine, it's in the air.

I am worthy of every dream I hold,
I am courageous, I am bold.
I am ready to receive, to take my stand,
The world is mine, within my hands.

Every challenge, I face with grace,
I grow stronger with every pace.
I am resilient, I rise above,
I trust the timing, I trust the love.

Send me the winds, send me the sun,
The universe whispers, "It's already done."
Watch it unfold, as I take my stand,
The world is mine, within my hands.

I am worthy, I am enough,
I am capable, I am tough.
I am the creator of my fate,
Everything I need comes when I wait.

So, Universe send me the sun and moon your way,
For I know, today's the day.